Wander the World with Warm-Ups

40 Fun Warm-Ups Using Songs from 20 Countries

By Lynn M. Brinckmeyer

T0056033

Shawnee Press

EXCLUSIVELY DISTRIBUTED BY

HAL•LEONARD®
CORPORATION

7777 W. BLUEMOUND RD. P.O. BOX 13819 MILWAUKEE, WI 53213

In Australia Contact:
Hal Leonard Australia Pty. Ltd.
4 Lentara Court
Cheltenham, Victoria, 3192 Australia
Email: ausadmin@halleonard.com.au

Visit Shawnee Press online at **www.shawneepress.com**
Visit Hal Leonard online at **www.halleonard.com**

Table of Contents

Overview 4

AUSTRIA
Glockenjodler 6

CANADA
Land of the Silver Birch 7

CZECHOSLOVAKIA
Ifca's Castle 8

DENMARK
Clapping Land 9

FRANCE
French Folk Song 10

GHANA
Obwisana 12

ISRAEL
Artza Alinu 13
Hevenu Shalom Aleichem 14
Hineh Ma Tov 15
S'vivon 16

JAPAN
Kaeru No Uta 17
Kagome 18

LESOTHO
Thula, Thula, Ngoana 19

LIBERIA
Kokoleoko 20

MEXICO
Caballito Blanco 21
Fray Martin 22

NETHERLANDS
Sarasponda 23

NEW ZEALAND
Epo I Tai Tai E. 24

NIGERIA
Funwa Alafia. 25
Eh Soom Boo Kawaya .26
Ise Oluwa. 27

RUSSIA
Vesper Hymn 28

SOUTH AFRICA
Mangoane mpulele. 29

SWEDEN
Ritsch, Ratsch 30

TRINIDAD
Boysie. 31

UNITED STATES
In That Great Gittin' Up Mornin' 32
Neesa, Neesa 34
Oh, Freedom. 35
Standin' in the Need of Prayer. 36

ZAIRE
Kee-Chee. 38

GENERAL WARM-UPS. **39**
Chromatic Scale 40
Communicate! 41
Counting Canon 42
Count in 10 Languages .44
For Health and Strength 45
I Have Rhythm 46
Pentatonic Melody. 47
Pat, Clap 48
Skip to My Lou 49
Cindy 50
Li'l Liza Jane. 50
Pepperoni Pizza. 51
What Shall I Do Today?. 52

About the Writer 53

Overview

Every school day, choral directors across the country begin their rehearsals with a series of warm-up exercises that are intended to prepare their students' bodies and minds for a focused and energetic rehearsal. I often use canons and short folk songs from other cultures to add variety to the warm-up process. Students learn most simple, repetitive folk songs quite easily. Consequently, advanced musical concepts such as tone quality, articulation, blend and part independence can be addressed without getting overwhelmed by unfamiliar text. Teachers may use the folk songs, canons and rhythm activities in this book to take their students on a vocal journey of world music. Remember, many cultures learn songs in the oral tradition and move whenever they sing. And, whenever we sing a song from another culture, it is a merging of traditions and backgrounds.

The purpose of this book is to serve as a resource with songs from a variety of countries. This book also serves as a guidebook by presenting ideas and strategies to use these songs in either choral ensemble or classroom settings. All of the songs, canons and rhythm activities presented may be substituted for traditional warm-ups. Songs and activities in this book are listed according to their respective country of origin. Included are step-by-step guidelines and user-friendly strategies to engage both beginning students and more advanced singers.

In addition to using these resources for warm-ups, many of them also work in the following situations:

- Sing a canon at the beginning of the first rehearsal to create immediate success in making music; focus on producing a lovely tone, with phrasing and harmony.
- Sing short folk songs or canons to keep students on task during transitions between songs or activities, or when putting materials away.
- Sing songs or canons when moving groups of students from place to place.
- During the final minutes of class, sing a canon or folk song to provide a musical moment and foster a community of singers.
- Create an opportunity for students to experience a little victory or success. Sing a simple canon or folk song between challenging activities to build in an energy break.
- Use short songs or melodies for solo auditions or chamber ensemble auditions.

Most of the teaching strategies proposed for each of the songs and activities in this book are interchangeable with most of the other songs or warm-ups. All of the songs, activities and recommended lesson ideas align with the recently updated National Core Arts Standards. The standards were developed by the National Coalition for Core Arts Standards and can be accessed on the website: **http://nccas.wikispaces.com/Conceptual+Framework.**

Teachers of all subjects generate opportunities and experiences for their students to learn how to function in life. Because of the unique aspects of music, we can create a community of learners in our ensembles. We music educators are incredibly fortunate to have music as a prominent force in our lives, and I hope that teachers use this book to provide meaningful experiences for singers.

Acknowledgements

Dr. George Heller, an influential professor at The University of Kansas, ignited my curiosity to learn as much as I could about other cultures through their music. I am grateful for his guidance.

Thank you to Will Schmid for continuing to feed and educate my passion for world music.

Thank you, Greg Gilpin for providing me this opportunity to share songs and activities I've learned during my travels to 48 states and numerous countries across the globe.

Finally, I am grateful to my family, my colleagues and students who continue to teach me how to be a better human and musician.

 # How To Access Pronunciation Guide

1. To access content in Hal Leonard's MY LIBRARY, go to **www.halleonard.com/mylibrary**.

2. Follow the instructions to set up your own My Library account, so that codes are saved for future access, and you don't have to re-enter them every time.

3. Once you have created your own library account, then enter the 16-digit product code listed on page 1.

4. This PDF file can be viewed online or downloaded to your computer.

AUSTRIA

Glockenjodler

Austrian Folk Song

Hol - la - ri, Hol - la - ro, Hol - la - ri - di ri - di - o. Hol - la -

ri, Hol - la - ro, Hol - la - ri - di ri - di - o.

English Translation

Bell Yodler (nonsense syllables to sound like a bell)

Teaching Ideas

- Chant the text while stepping the beat in cut time.
  - Use a slow tempo.
- Sing the song while focusing on unified vowels.
  - Strive for a pure, bell-like tone.
- Divide the class into 2 sections. Take turns singing each phrase.

Advanced Extensions

- Challenge students to create their own harmony to the song.
- Invite the students to try singing the song in a 2-part canon.
- Part 2 starts when Part 1 sings the two-note pickup to the second line.
- Sing it again as a canon, entering after the first 2 beats.

CANADA

Land of the Silver Burch

Canadian Folk Song

Land of the sil - ver birch, home of the bea - ver,

Where still the migh - ty moose wan-ders at will.

Blue lake and rock - y shore, I will re - turn once more.

Boom did - dy boom boom, boom did - dy boom, boom,

boom did - dy boom, boom boom.

Teaching Ideas

- Tap the rhythm and chant the text.
- Sing the pitches on a neutral syllable.
- Have singers create an ostinato and sing it with the song.
- Clap every time you sing the pitch *F*.
- Sing every other measure. (Ex. Sing mea.1, audiate mea.2, etc.)
- Sing the song and leave out/audiate all text on the pitch *A*.
- Try leaving out pitches other than *A*.

Advanced Extensions

- Figure out the solfége for this minor key.
- Sing the song in a canon, entering after two measures.
  - Sing it again in a canon, entering after 2 beats.
  - Sing once more, entering after 1 beat.
- Add the ostinati while singing the song in a canon in 2 parts, then 3 parts, then 4 parts.

CZECHOSLOVAKIA

Ifca's Castle

Czech Folk Song

A - bove the plain of gold and green, A
young boy's head is plain - ly seen; A
hu - ya, hu - ya, hu - ya - ya, Swift - ly flow - ing riv - er. A
hu - ya, hu - ya, hu - ya - ya, Swift - ly flow - ing riv - er.

Teaching Ideas

- Share the pulse by tapping the beat lightly and chanting the text.
- Sing the melody on a neutral syllable.
  - Remember to sing with increased breath energy through the note(s) BEFORE the high pitches.

Advanced Extensions

- Sing the song using different style periods, with different accompaniment patterns. For ex: in the styles of Bach, Mozart, Brahms, and Wagner; in the styles of gospel, country and jazz.
- Have groups of students stand in the four corners of the room. Are you listening to each other to share the pulse and unify the vowels?
- Sing the song with a very bright tone, swallowed tone, strident tone, cool and pure tone, warm and resonant tone.
  - Discuss the different tone qualities and vocal production needed for each of the different timbres.
  - Have students decide which tone quality is most appropriate for this song and model that by singing it for the class.

DENMARK

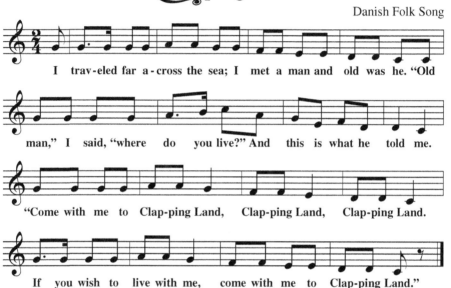

Clapping Land

Danish Folk Song

I trav-eled far a-cross the sea; I met a man and old was he. "Old man," I said, "where do you live?" And this is what he told me. "Come with me to Clap-ping Land, Clap-ping Land, Clap-ping Land. If you wish to live with me, come with me to Clap-ping Land."

Teaching Ideas

- Step the beat and chant the text.
- Sing the song on solfége syllables, using hand signs.
- Sing the pitches on a neutral syllable and snap on each anacrusis.
- Sing the song and clap each time you sing the words *clapping land*.

Advanced Extensions

- Have students create new words and actions.
  - Example: stomping land, skipping land, etc.
- Divide the class into two groups.
  - Group A sings lines 1 and 2, then Group B sings lines 3 and 4.
  - Group A sings lines 1 and 2 as a partner song, while Group B sings lines 3 and 4.
- Sing the song as a canon, entering 2 beats apart.

FRANCE

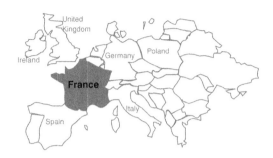

French Folk Song

Dans le ciel je suis prêt à____ vo - ler,

Oub - lie l'a - vion, c'est a - vec une fus - ée

Vive les é - toi - les et la lune é - clai - rée

C'est ma fus - ée qui peut m'y trans - por - ter

Trois, deux, un, ma fus - ée vole dans le ciel!

English Translation

In the sky I'm ready to fly,
Forget the plane, it is with a rocket,
Bright stars and moon lit,
This is my rocket that can carry me there,
Three, two, one, my rocket flying in the sky!

Teaching Ideas

- Sing the pitches on solfége, using hand signs.
- Sing the pitches on solfége in a canon, entering two measures apart.
- Sing, then audiate, every other measure on solfége. Continue to use the hand signs when audiating.
- Divide the class into two groups.
  - Group A sings measures 1, 3, 5, etc. Group B sings measures 2, 4, 6, etc.

Advanced Extensions

- Sing the song on solfége with hand signs, and leave out/audiate different pitches. (For ex. Leave out all text on the pitch *A*.)
- Challenge the students to sing the song on solfége, with hand signs, in a canon, entering after three beats, then after 1 beat.
- Chant the French text.
  - Discuss how the rhythm must change to adapt to the French text.
  - Sing the song with the French text.
  - Sing the French text in a canon.
- Practice singing the pitches on mixed vowels used in foreign languages.
  - Examples: [ö], [œ], [y], [ü].

GHANA

Obwisana

Child's Game Song

Ob - wi - sa - na   sa   na - na,   Ob - wi - sa - na   sa,

Ob - wi - sa - na   sa   na - na,   Ob - wi - sa - na   sa.

English Translation

The rock crushed my hand.

Teaching Ideas

- Learn the song in the oral tradition: The teacher sings it several times and students join in when they are ready.
- Sing the song at different tempos.
- Sing the song beginning with a very slow tempo and gradually speeding up with each rendition.
- Sing the song beginning with a very quick tempo and gradually slow down with each rendition.
- Create body percussion, clapping/passing movements for the song.

Advanced Extensions

- Try singing the song in a canon, entering after 1 measure.
- Sing the song as a canon again, entering after 2 beats, then entering after 1 beat.
- Have all of the voices sing at individual tempos, coming together at the end of each phrase, then hold the final syllable until every voice has arrived at that syllable.
- Try singing the song in two or more different keys at the same time. For example: C Major, E Major and G Major.

ISRAEL

Artza Alinu

Israeli Dance

Art - za a - li - nu, Art - sa a - li - nu, Art - za a - li - nu.

K' - var cha - rash - nu v' - gam za - ra - nu,

A - vod od lo kat - zar - nu.

English Translation

We ascended to the Land,
We've already ploughed and sown, too,
but we have not yet reaped.

Teaching Ideas

- Step the beat and clap/chant the rhythm.
- Have students locate all of the measures that contain syncopated rhythms.
- Sing the song as written.
- Slow the tempo down.
  - Sing all of the words, except clap and audiate all text on the pitch *F*.
  - Audiate and clap on different words or syllables.

Advanced Extensions

- Invite students to sing the song in two groups.
  - Group B enters after Group A has sung line 1 two times.
- Challenge students to sing the song in a canon, entering 2 beats apart.
- Challenge students to sing the song in a canon, entering 1 measure apart.

ISRAEL

Hevenu Shalom Aleichem

Israeli Folk Song

He - ve - nu sha - lom a' - ley-chem, He - ve - nu

sha - lom a' - ley - chem, He - ve - nu

sha - lom a' - ley - chem, He - ve - nu

sha - lom, sha - lom, sha - lom a' - ley - chem.

English Translation

Peace be with you where you go.
Peace be with you my friend.

Teaching Ideas

- Sing the song on a neutral syllable until the melody is learned.
- Speak the text while tapping the rhythm.
- Begin singing with a very slow tempo and increase the tempo throughout the song.

Advanced Extensions

- Have the students stand in a circle.
  - Pass the song around the circle.
  - One student sings the first word, the next in line sings the second word, etc.
  - Try the same exercise in a canon. Pass the song around, and begin a 2nd part entering after the first phrase is completed.

ISRAEL

Hineh Ma Tov

Israeli Folk Song

Hi-neh ma tov u-ma na' - im   She-vet a-chim gam ya - chad.

Hi - neh   ma   tov She - vet a-chim gam   ya - chad.

Hi - neh   ma   tov She - vet a-chim gam   ya - chad.

English Translation

How good and pleasant it is
For brothers and sisters to sit together.

Teaching Ideas

- Count out loud to 6 and clap on beats 4 and 6.
  - Repeat this over and over to get comfortable with the 6/8 meter.
  - Count silently and clap on beats 4 and 6.
  - Change up the beats to 2 and 5; 1, 3 and 4, etc.
- Sizzle the rhythm of the words on one breath for each phrase to help build endurance, phrasing and dynamics.
- Sing the pitches on a neutral syllable.
- Chant the text.
- Sing the song with the text.

Advanced Extensions

- Stand in a circle and have the students face the outside of the circle.
  - Sing the song and strive to listen for every other singer in order to share the pulse and unify the vowels.
- Continue facing outside the circle.
  - Have three students stand in the center of the circle.
  - Silently direct one of them to sing the song as a solo.
  - Ask the other choir members to identify the soloist.
  - Discuss vocal timbres and individual characteristics of different voices.

ISRAEL

S'vivon

Israeli Folk Song

S' - vi - von,   sov sov sov,   Cha - nu - kah_____ hu - chag tow.

Cha - nu - kah   hu - chag tov   S' - vi - von__   sov sov sov.

Nes ga - dol__   ha - ya   po, __   Nes ga - dol ha - ya__   sham. __

Nes go - dal ha - ya   sham, __   chag sim - chah__   hu   la   am.

English Translation

Spinning top, spin, spin, spin.
Chanukah is a great holiday.
A happy holiday for everyone,
A great miracle happened there.

Teaching Ideas

- Learn all parts of the song on a neutral pitch.
- Speak the Hebrew pronunciation.
- Sing the Hebrew text and snap on the accidentals.
- Sing the verse and chorus as partner songs.
- Invite soloists to sing different lines of the song.
- Sing the English translation.

Advanced Extensions

- Figure out the solfége for this minor key and sing it with hand signs.
- Have two groups sing the song.
  - One group will sing in English and the other group will sing the Hebrew at the same time.
  - Sing the song in English as a canon concurrently with another group singing a canon in Hebrew.

JAPAN

Kaeru No Uta

Japanese Folk Song

Ka - e - ru no u - ta ga Ki - ko - e - te Ku - ru - yo

Gwa, gwa, gwa, gwa, Ge - ro, ge - ro, ge - ro, ge - ro, Gwa, gwa, gwa.

English Translation

The frog's song, we can hear it (frog noises).

Teaching Ideas

- Two finger clap the rhythm while chanting rhythm syllables.
- Sing the song on solfége, using hand signs.
- Speak the text and snap on all of the rests.
- Sing the song with the Japanese text.

Advanced Extensions

- Sing the song in a canon, entering 2 measures apart.
  - Try singing the song in a canon, entering 2 beats apart.
  - Sing the song again as a canon again, entering 1 beat apart.
- Add body percussion.
  - Clap on all quarter notes.
  - Stomp on every half note.
  - Snap on every rest.
  - Pat thighs, alternating hands for the eighth notes.
- Sing the song with body percussion.
- Perform the song with body percussion, while audiating the song.
- Perform the song with body percussion, while audiating in a canon.

JAPAN

Kagome

Japanese Children's Game

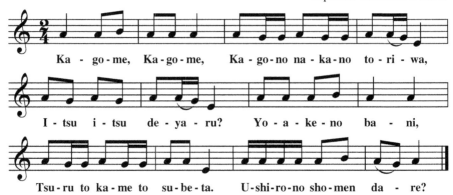

Ka - go - me, Ka - go - me, Ka - go - no na - ka - no to - ri - wa,

I - tsu i - tsu de - ya - ru? Yo - a - ke - no ba - ni,

Tsu - ru to ka - me to su - be - ta. U - shi - ro - no sho - men da - re?

English Translation

Bird in a basket,
When will it come out? From morn till night,
Misfortune coming, the person who stands behind.

Teaching Ideas

- Identify which measures share the same rhythm patterns.
- Locate which measures include sixteenth notes.
- Chant and tap the rhythm syllables for the song.
- Sing the pitches on solfége with hand signs.
- Chant the Japanese text.
  - Have half of the class clap the rhythm while the other half sings the song on the Japanese text.
  - Trade parts and sing/clap again.

Advanced Extensions

- Sing the song on solfége with hand signs.
  - Assign one group to sing only the pitches on eighth notes.
  - Have the other group sing all of the other pitches.
  - Trade parts and sing the song again.
- Sing the song with the Japanese text.
  - Pay attention to the details such as the smaller notes. Sing them as carefully as all of the other pitches.
- Sing the song in two or more voice parts, with each voice part starting on a different pitch. For example: *F♯, A, C.*
  - Discuss the challenges of singing with different starting pitches at the same time.
  - What skills are being developed with this exercise?

LESOTHO

Thula, Thula, Ngoana

African Folk Song

Thu - la, thu - la, ngoa - na, __ Thu - la, thu - la, ngoa - na, __

Thu - la, thu - la, ngoa - na, __ Thu - la, thu - la, ngoa - na. __

English Translation

Hush, hush child.

Teaching Ideas

- Have students close their eyes and listen as the teacher sings the song several times.
- Sing the song with the teacher.
- Invite several volunteers to sing the song for the class.

Advanced Extensions

- Sing the song with an average tone quality and musicality, then sing it with a beautiful tone and advanced musicality.
- Assess by talking to a neighbor and telling them 2 things that were different between the two performances.
- Sing the song with a hooty tone, a bright tone and a nasal tone.
- Sing the song with a warm, resonant tone.
- Try singing the song as a canon, entering 4 measures apart.
  - Sing the song as a canon again, entering 2 measures apart, then entering 1 measure apart, then entering 2 beats apart.

LIBERIA

Kokoleoko

Traditional Liberian Folk Song

Ko - ko - le - o - ko,   Ma - ma,   Ko - ko - le - o - ko,

Ko - ko - le - o - ko,   chick - en   crow - ing   to - day.

English Translation

Chicken crowing today.

Teaching Ideas

- Step the beat while tapping the rhythm lightly.
- Sing the pitches on a neutral syllable, and clap on the rests.
- Chant the text.
- Ask for volunteers to sing the song.
- Sing the song with the text.
- Insert different student's names for *Mama*.

Advanced Extensions

- Sing, then audiate, every other measure.
- Sing all of the pitches except *A*.
- Sing every other word.
- Add body percussion.
    - Stomp on all of the eighth notes.
    - Clap on all of the quarter notes.
    - Snap on all of the rests.
- Perform the song without singing, using only body percussion.

Mexico

Caballito Blanco

Traditional Children's Folk Song

Ca - bal - li - to   blan - co   sa - ca - me   de   a - qui,___

Lle - va - me   a   mi   pueb - lo   don - de - yo   na - ci.

English Translation

White horse take me away from here
Take me to the town where I was born.

Teaching Ideas

- Teacher sings the song several times.
- Students hum along when they are familiar with the melody.
- Chant the Spanish text.
- Have students sing the song with a neighbor to check their understanding.
- Ask for volunteers to sing the Spanish text for the class.
- Have the class sing the song with the Spanish text.
- Create different body percussion for eighth notes, quarter notes and half notes.
- Sing the song with body percussion.

Advanced Extensions

- Sing the song as a canon, entering after 3 beats.
- Sing the song as a canon, using body percussion.
- Perform the body percussion as a canon, without singing.
- Sing the song as a canon.
    - Use two groups.
    - One voice part sings in the Key of C Major.
    - The second group sings in the Key of E Major.
    - Add a third group singing in the Key of G Major.

Mexico

Fray Martin

Latin American Folk Song

Fray Mar - tin al cam - pan - a - rio,

Su - be_y to - ca la cam - pan - a,

Tan! Tan! Tan! Tan!

English Translation

Brother Martin to the bell tower,
Go up and touch the bell.
Ding, dong, ding, dong.

Teaching Ideas

- Clap the rhythm while chanting the rhythm syllables.
- Sing the solfége syllables using hand signs.
- Speak the Spanish text.
- Sing the song with the Spanish text.
- Sing the song as a canon, entering 4 measures apart.

Advanced Extensions

- Sing all of the pitches using solfége, and hand signs.
    - Audiate the quarter notes while using the hand signs.
- Sing every other measure on the Spanish text.
- Sing the entire song except, leave out/audiate all of the pitches on F♯.
- Divide the class into two groups:
    - Part A sings measures 1, 3, 5, etc.
    - Part B sings measures 2, 4, 6, etc.

NETHERLANDS

Sarasponda

Dutch Folk Song

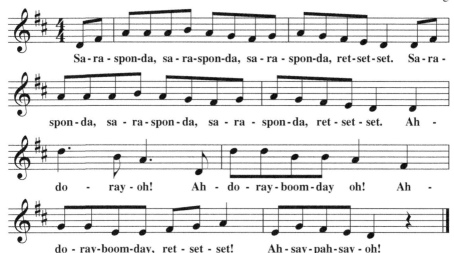

Sa-ra-spon-da, sa-ra-spon-da, sa-ra-spon-da, ret-set-set. Sa-ra-

spon-da, sa-ra-spon-da, sa-ra-spon-da, ret-set-set. Ah-

do - ray-oh! Ah - do-ray-boom-day oh! Ah-

do-ray-boom-day, ret-set-set! Ah-say-pah-say-oh!

English Translation

(Nonsense Syllables)

Teaching Ideas

- Clap the rhythm, paying special attention to the rests.
- Sing the pitches on solfége syllables with hand signs.
- Sing the song with the text.

Advanced Extensions

- Sing the song on a neutral syllable and leave out the words that fall on the pitch A.
- Sing the song on the text and leave out the words on the pitch $F\sharp$.
- Try leaving out other pitches.
- Sing lines 1 and 2 as a partner song with lines 3 and 4.
- Sing the song as a canon, entering 1 measure apart, then entering 2 beats apart.
- Create several ostinati to sing with the song.
- Transfer the ostinati to body percussion and perform them with the song.

NEW ZEALAND

Epo I Tai Tai E

Maori Song

E-po i tai tai e, O e-po i tai tai e.

E-po i tai tai e-po i tu-ki tu-ki,

e-po i tu-ki tu-ki e.

English Translation

A strong man fights like a bull.

Teaching Ideas

- Tap your neighbor's shoulder and keep the beat while the teacher recites the text.
- Tap your neighbor's shoulder and keep the beat while the teacher teaches the song through echo/response.
- Two-finger clap the beat while singing the song.
- Create body percussion to go along with the song.
- Leave out/audiate different phrases of the song, while performing the body percussion.
- Audiate the entire song, while performing the body percussion.

Advanced Extensions

- Challenge students to sing this song as a canon, entering 4 beats apart.
  - Try to sing a canon again, entering 2 beats apart, then entering 1 beat apart.
- Sing the song as a canon and have each voice part leave out/audiate a different phrase.
- Sing the song and change the vocal timbre: silky, strident, warm, lifeless or cool.
- Pair up with a neighbor and discuss the differences in the sounds of the various timbres.
  - Discuss what a singer needs to do vocally to produce the different types of timbre/tone quality.

NIGERIA

Funwa Alafia

Yuroba Children's Song

Fun - wa   a - la - fi - a,   ash - ey,   ash - ey.

Fun - wa   a - la - fi - a,   ash - ey,   ash - ey.

English Translation

We welcome you.

Teaching Ideas

- Learn the song using the oral tradition.
  - Teacher sings it several times, then students repeat.
- Clap the rhythm.
- Discuss where the syncopated rhythms are located in the song.
- Ask for volunteers to sing the song with the Yuroba text.
- Sing the song again and strive to unify vowels.

Advanced Extensions

- Break into pairs and figure out the solfége and hand signs for the song. Then sing the song on solfége, using hand signs.
- Sing every other measure on solfége.
  - Example: Sing measure #1, audiate measure #2, etc.
- Sing the song, using the Yuroba text, in a canon.
  - Have each voice part enter 4 beats apart.
  - Try singing a canon entering 2 beats apart, then entering 1 beat apart.
- Have students stand in a circle.
  - Each person sings alone.
  - Start the canon, entering 2 beats apart, and go around the entire circle until everyone is singing.

NIGERIA

Eh Soom Boo Kawaya

Traditional Nigerian Boat Song

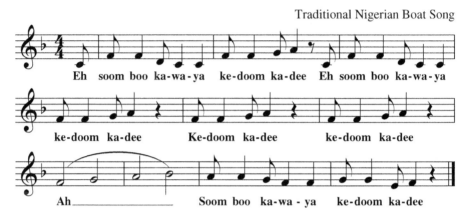

English Translation

The clouds are gathering; paddle faster.

Teaching Ideas

- Locate all of the measures that contain syncopated rhythms.
- Talk to your neighbor and clap the rhythm patterns together.
- Sing the pitches on a neutral syllable.
- Divide the class into two groups.
    - Have one group chant the text while the other group sings the pitches on a neutral syllable.
    - Trade parts and sing/chant the song again.
- Sing the song with the text.

Advanced Extensions

- Sing the song with the text.
    - Clap each time you sing a syncopated rhythm.
    - Add a small group of students who snap on each anacrusis.
    - Audiate the song while simultaneously clapping and snapping.
- Students stand in a circle.
    - Go around the circle, with each person singing a phrase of the song.
    - Turn and face outside the circle and have each person sing a phrase around the circle.

NIGERIA

Ise Oluwa

Nigerian Folk Song

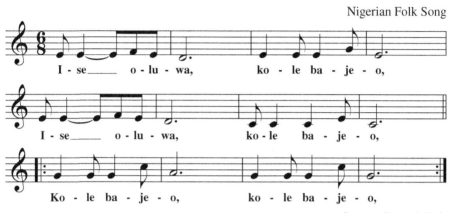

I - se____ o - lu - wa, ko - le ba - je - o,

I - se____ o - lu - wa, ko - le ba - je - o,

Ko - le ba - je - o, ko - le ba - je - o,

Repeat lines 1 & 2

English Translation

What God has made cannot be undone.

Teaching Ideas

- Gently step the big beats and tap the eighth note subdivision while the teacher hums the melody.
  - Students join the teacher and sing the melody on a neutral syllable.
- Pronounce the text.
- Sing the song call and response.
  - Teacher sings the first phrase as a call.
  - Student echo reply with the response.
  - Have half of the class sing the call, the other half sings the response.
  - Trade parts and sing the song again.

Advanced Extensions

- Create harmony lines to accompany the responses.
- Talk with a partner and create gentle body percussion or movement that works with the melody and the meaning of the text.
- Have volunteers demonstrate and teach the body percussion/movement to the class.
- Sing the song with the body percussion/movement.
- Invite different soloists to sing the call.

RUSSIA

Russia

Finland
Kazakhstan
Mongolia

Vesper Hymn

Text by Thomas Moore   Russian Melody

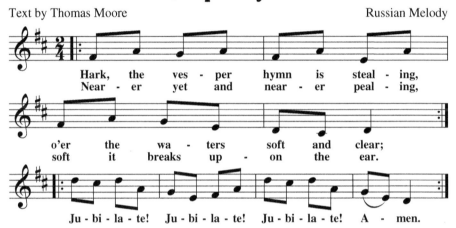

Hark, the ves - per hymn is steal - ing,
Near - er yet and near - er peal - ing,

o'er the wa - ters soft and clear;
soft it breaks up - on the ear.

Ju - bi - la - te! Ju - bi - la - te! Ju - bi - la - te! A - men.

Teaching Ideas
- Use hand signs and lip-sync the silent solfége for the song.
- Sing the song on solfége syllables, using hand signs.
- Divide the class into two groups.
  - Group A sings the solfége at the same time Group B sings the words.
  - Have the groups trade parts and sing the song again.
- Sing the song with the text.

Advanced Extensions
- Sing the song as a partner song.
  - Group A sings lines 1 and 2; Group B sings lines 3 and 4.
  - Have the groups trade parts and sing the song again.
- Sing the song as a canon, entering 2 beats apart.
- Sing the song in unison and use the wave to practice dynamics.
  - Start the wave on one side of the choir.
  - When students stand and wave their arms up, they increase their volume.
  - When students sit down, they decrease their volume.
  - Students sing *piano* when sitting and *forte* when standing.
  - Challenge the singers to sing the song in a canon, while using the wave to indicate dynamics.

SOUTH AFRICA

Mangoane mpulele

Traditional Sotho Rain Song

Ma - ngoa-ne mpu - le - le ke ne loa-ke pu - la Ma-ngoa ne,

Ma - ngoa-ne mpu - le - le ke ne loa-ke pu - la, Le

Fine

ha-di le pe-di le ha-di - le-tha-ro ke-nya-la mo-sa - di, mo-sa - di, Le

D. C. al Fine

ha - di le pe-di le ha - di - le-tha-ro ke-nya-la mo-sa - di.

English Translation

Aunt, open the door for me, I am getting wet with rain.
Whether it is here, whether it is there, I am getting wet with rain.

Teaching Ideas

- Work with a neighbor and clap the rhythm for the song.
- Set up the key by singing *do, mi, sol* in F Major.
  - Silently audiate the solfége with hand signs.
  - Check with your neighbor to make sure you both agree on the solfége and hand signs.
  - Sing the song on solfége syllables with hand signs.

Advanced Extensions

- Chant the text.
- Sing the song on the text.
- Create harmony lines for the song and sing it with harmony.
- Try singing the song as a canon entering 1 measure apart.
  - Sing the song as a canon again, adding harmony to each part.

SWEDEN

Ritsch, Ratsch

Swedish Children's Song

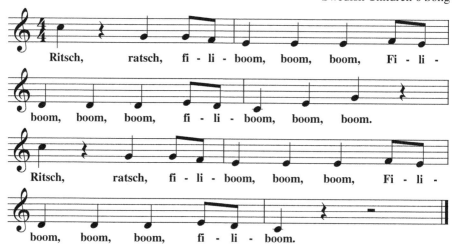

English Translation

Snip, snap (nonsense words)

Teaching Ideas

- Tap the beat on the shoulder of a neighbor and speak the text in rhythm.
- Sing the song at different tempos.
- Create body percussion for each of the words.

Advanced Extension

- Sing the song in a canon, entering 2 measures apart, then again entering 1 measure apart.
- Sing the song and leave out all of the words or syllables on the pitch *D*.
- Sing the song and leave out different words/pitches.
  - Substitute the body percussion for the words.
  - Leave out an additional word each time you sing the song.
- Perform the song with only body percussion.
- Perform the song in a canon with only body percussion.

TRINIDAD

Boysie

Trinidad Lullaby
As sung to the author by Danton Bankay

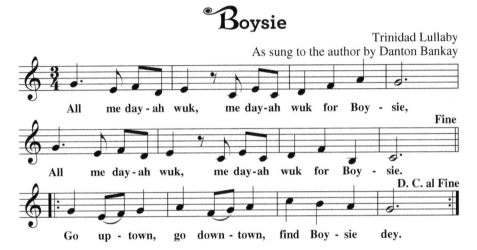

All me day-ah wuk, me day-ah wuk for Boy - sie,

Fine

All me day-ah wuk, me day-ah wuk for Boy - sie.

D. C. al Fine

Go up - town, go down - town, find Boy - sie dey.

English Translation

All my day I work for Boysie,
Go up town, go downtown find Boysie there.

Teaching Ideas

- Step the beat while the teacher chants the words.
- Have half of the students tap the beat, while the other students tap the rhythm.
  - Have the students trade parts while lip-syncing the words.
- Sing the song with the words.
- Have the two groups take turns singing different phrases.

Advanced Extensions

- Have two groups take turns singing every other word.
- Assign the word *Boysie* to a small group. The rest of the students sing all the words except for *Boysie*. Sing the song with the two groups, then trade parts and sing it again.
- Sing the song in a canon.
  - Enter 2 measures apart.
  - Enter 1 measure apart.
- Sing lines 1 and 2 as a partner song with lines 3 and 4.

UNITED STATES

In That Great Gittin' Up Mornin'

Traditional Spiritual

(swing eighths)

In that great git-tin' up morn-in' fare thee well,

fare thee well; In that great git-tin' up

morn-in' fare thee well, fare thee well; I'm go-in'

Fine

tell you 'bout the com-in' of a new day, Fare thee well,

fare thee well. I'm go-in' tell you 'bout the com-in' of a

D.S. al Fine

new day, Fare thee well, fare thee well. In that

Teaching Ideas

- While sitting, tap heels lightly to the beat and chant the words.
- Figure out the solfége syllables, then sing the solfége with hand signs.
- Sing the song with the words.

Advanced Extensions

- Sing the song on solfége syllables with hand signs.
    - Leave out all of the *sol* syllables.
    - Add other syllables to leave out/audiate.
- Divide the class into two groups.
    - Group A sings the words *fare thee well*.
    - Group B sings all of the other words.
    - Trade parts and sing it again.
- Sing the song as a canon, entering two beats apart.
- Sing lines 1 and 2 as a partner song with lines 3 and 4.
- Create a harmony line for the song.

UNITED STATES

Neesa, Neesa

Seneca Chant

Nee - sa, Nee - sa, Nee - sa, Nee - sa, Nee - sa, Nee - sa,

Nee-sa, Nee-sa, Nee - sa, Gai - we - oh. _____ Gai - we - oh. _____

English Translation

Honor the creator of the winter moon in January.

Teaching Ideas

- Teach the song in the oral tradition.
    - Teacher sings the entire song several times.
    - Students join in when they have learned it.
- Sing the song, listening for pure vowel unification and perfect intonation.
    - Sing the song at different dynamic levels.

Advanced Extensions

- Challenge the students to sing the song in a canon.
    - Enter 4 beats apart.
    - Enter 2 beats apart.
    - Enter 1 beat apart.
- Have the singers stand in a circle around the room.
    - Divide the circle into 8 parts.
    - Sing the song in a canon, entering 2 beats apart.
    - Challenge the students to sing alone and sing the song as a canon, entering 1 beat apart around the circle. Keep singing until everyone has sung the song several times.
    - Conduct while the students are singing the canon, changing dynamic levels as they sing.

United States

Oh, Freedom

Spiritual

Oh,_____ free-dom! Oh,_____ free-dom!

Oh, free-dom o-ver me._____ And be-

fore I'd be a slave,__ I'll be bur-ied in my grave. And go

home to my Lord__ and be free._____

Teaching Ideas

- Locate the syncopated rhythm patterns in the song.
- Sing the song using solfége syllables and hand signs.
- Sing the song with the words.
- Start with a very slow tempo.

Advanced Extensions

- Listen to various recordings of the song.
- Sing the song at different tempos.
  - Discuss how the character of the song changes when the tempo is quicker or slower.
  - Which tempo is appropriate to share the message of the text?
- Show photos of slaves. Discuss the physical and emotional challenges slaves faced.
- Sing lines 1 and 2 as a partner song with lines 3 and 4.
- Create harmony lines to go with the song.

UNITED STATES

Standin' in the Need of Prayer

(swing eighths) 𝄋

Traditional Spiritual

It's me, it's me, it's me, O Lord, __ stand-in' in the need of prayer. __ It's me, it's me, it's me, O Lord, __ stand-in' in the need of prayer. __

Fine

Not my moth - er, not my fa - ther, but it's me, O Lord, __ stand - in' in the need of prayer. __ Not my moth - er, not my fa - ther, but it's me, O Lord, __

D.S. al Fine

stand - in' in the need of prayer. __ It's

Teaching Ideas

- Speak the text while lightly tapping the beat.
- Speak the text and place the syllabic stress on the 'wrong' syllables:
  - Example: *stand-IN; pray-ER.*
  - Discuss with a neighbor where the proper syllabic stress should occur in the words to this song.
- Sing the song using the correct syllabic stress.
- Invite students to sing the verse as a solo or small ensemble.
- Break into pairs to create new verses.
  - *It's not my brother.*
  - *It's not my kitty.*
  - *It's not my puppy.*
  - *It's not my doctor.*
  - *It's not my lawyer.*
- Have students teach their new verses to the class.

Advanced Extensions

- Tap the dotted sixteenth rhythm pattern with your neighbor.
- Sing every other measure.
- Sing every other word.
- Create harmonies that work with the song.
- Teach the new harmony lines to the class.

ZAIRE

Kee Chee

Folk Song from Zaire

Ah wu - ne ku - ne cha o wu - ni, Ah

wu - ne ku - ne cha o wu - ni,

Ah yi yi yi - ki ay kae ay - na,

Ah yi yi yi - ki ay kae ay - na,

Ah ooo_____ ah dee mee kee - chee.

Teaching Ideas

- Lightly tap the sternum while sizzling the rhythm.
- Identify the term *anacrusis* and locate each anacrusis in the song.
- Speak the text while tapping the rhythm.
  - Clap on the rests.
- Sing the song on solfége syllables, using hand signs.
- Sing the song with the text.

Advanced Extensions

- Divide the class into two groups.
  - Part A sing lines 1 and 3.
  - Part B sing lines 2 and 4.
  - All students sing line 5.
- Sing the song as a canon, entering 2 beats apart.

General Warm-Ups

General Warm-Ups

Chromatic Scale

Teaching Ideas

- Sing the pitches on a neutral syllable, accompanied by a keyboard/piano.
- Talk about the half steps in a chromatic scale.
  - Use a keyboard or visual aid.
- Sing the scale pattern on a neutral syllable without any accompaniment.

Advanced Extension

- Sing the scale pattern on solfége syllables with hand signs.
- Sing the scale pattern as a canon, using a neutral syllable or solfége syllables with hand signs.
- Change the straight quarter note rhythm patterns. For example: dotted quarter/eighth, eighth/dotted quarter, waltz rhythm.
- Add variety: staccato, legato, crescendo, decrescendo, two note phrases, etc.
- Sing the pitches on solfége syllables, with hand signs, in a canon entering 4 beats apart.
  - Try it in a canon entering 2 beats apart.
- Challenge singers to use solfége syllables with hand signs, and sing every other pitch.
  - Audiate the pitches that are left out.
  - Leave out different pitches such as *re* and *fa*.
  - Sing the scale pattern in a canon with each voice part leaving out different syllables.
- Sing the song in canon while each part starts on a different *do*.
  - Example: Part A begins in C major, part B begins in E major.
- Create texts to go along with the scale pattern, such as the A, B, Cs.
  - Sing the scale pattern in a canon and leave out different words in the new text.

General Warm-Ups

Communicate!

1

Let us sing!

2

You are my new B - F - F!

3

O - M - G, O - M - G. I love to sing!

4

L - O - L, it's time for choir!

Teaching Ideas

- Chant the phrases using various voice inflections.
  - Select a single phrase to focus on or chant them in succession.
- Sing the phrases on scale passages such as outlined above.
- Add physiology to enhance the tone or specific concepts.
- Figure out the solfége for each message.
- Silent solfége using hand signs for each message.
- Sing the phrases on solfége syllables using hand signs.

Advanced Extensions

- Invite students to pair up and create their own messages.
  - Perform the new messages for the other students.
  - Teach the new messages to the class and have the class sing along.
- Ask the students to figure out if any of the newly created messages can be performed together as partner songs.
- Perform the partner messages together.

General Warm-Ups

Counting Canon

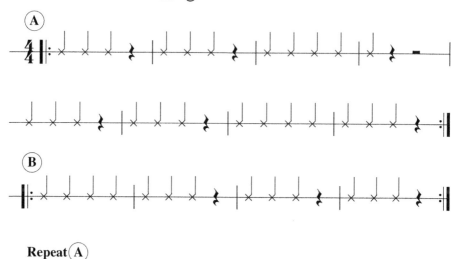

Repeat (A)

Body Percussion

1. Extend arms out front, chest high. **Clap** hands once then **tap** lightly on the sternum/chest with the right hand, then left hand.
2. **Pat** thighs with alternating hands.
3. Arms across chest like a genie for **down** position. Bring hands up so that the backs of hands tap for **up** position.
4. **Stomp** twice with right leg, then stomp twice with left leg.

Movement Patterns

Clap, tap, tap; clap, tap, tap; clap, tap, tap, pat, pat (rest, rest).
Clap, tap, tap; clap, tap, tap; clap, tap, tap, pat, pat, stomp, stomp (rest).
      Repeat
Down, up, down, up, down, up, down.
Stomp, stomp, clap (rest). Stomp, stomp, clap (rest).
      Repeat
Clap, tap, tap; clap, tap, tap; clap, tap, tap, pat, pat (rest, rest).
Clap, tap, tap; clap, tap, tap; clap, tap, tap, pat, pat, stomp, stomp (rest).
      Repeat

Some components of the movements attributed to Sharon L. Morrow

Teaching Ideas

- Chant the movements while doing the body percussion.
- Leave out the words on the A section while doing the body percussion.
- Leave out the words on the A and B sections while doing the body percussion.
- Leave out the words on ABA except the final words *that's all!*

Advanced Extensions

- Perform the activities outlined above in a canon, entering 4 beats apart.
  - Try a canon entering 2 beats apart.
- Stand in a circle.
  - With one person on each part, chant the words while performing body percussion.
  - Perform the canon, entering 2 beats apart.
  - Do the same thing again with only body percussion and leave out the chanting, except everyone shouts *that's all* at the end.

General Warm-Ups

Count in 10 Languages

Teaching Ideas
- Sing the pitches on solfége with hand signs.
- Sing the pitches on numbers: 1, 2, 3, 4, 5, 6, 7, 8, 9, 10.
- Sing the exercise ascending or descending by half steps.
- Sing the exercise in different languages:
    - Spanish: *uno, dos, tres, cuatro, cinco, seis, siete, ocho, nueve, diez.*
    - French: *un, deux, trois, quatre, cinq, six, sept, huit, neuf, dix.*
    - Afrikaans: *een, twee, drie, vier, vyf, ses, sewe, agt, nege, tien.*
    - German: *eins, zwei, drei, vier, fünf, sechs, sieben, acht, neun, zehn.*
    - Italian: *uno, due, tre, quattro, cinque, sei, sette, otto, nove, dieci.*
    - Swahili: *moja, mbili, tatu, nne, tano, sita, saba, nane, tisa, kumi.*
    - Latin: *unus, duo, tres, quattuor, quinque, sex, septem, octo, novem, decem.*
    - Tagalog: *isa, dalawang, tatlong, apat, na lilmang, anim, na pitong, walong, siyam, na sampung.*
    - Swedish: *ett, två, tre, fyra, fem, sex, sju, åtta, nio, tio.*
    - Japanese: *ichi, ni, sahn, she, go, roku, shichi, hachi, kyuu, juu.*

Advanced Extensions
- Sing the exercise in a canon with each language.
- Sing two or more languages at the same time.
- Sing the exercise in a canon in two or more languages:
    - Have each voice part sing the pitches in a different language.

General Warm-Ups

For Health and Strength

Traditional

For health and strength and dai - ly bread, we

praise thy name oh Lord.

Teaching Ideas

- Sing the song on solfége syllables, using hand signs.
- Invite different students to sing the song as a solo.
- Sing the song in a canon, with each new voice part entering after 4 beats.
- Sing the song again focusing on articulation.
    - Ask for volunteers to demonstrate perfect diction while singing the song.

Advanced Extensions

- Have students translate the words into another language such as Spanish, French or German.
    - Invite students to teach their new words to the class.
    - Sing the song as a canon, with each voice part singing a different language.

General Warm-Ups

I Have Rhythm

Rhythmic phrase shared by Juan Cavazos

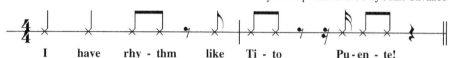

I   have   rhy - thm   like   Ti - to   Pu - en - te!

Teaching Ideas

- Chant the words while stepping the beat.
- Whisper the words while patting the beat lightly on the thighs.
- Use different voices while chanting the words. For example: British, Cowboy, Dracula, etc.
  - Chant the words again and snap on the rests.
- Use different students' names instead of Tito Puente.

Advanced Extensions

- Chant the words over and over.
  - Leave off a new syllable and audiate those words each time you chant.
  - For example, leave off:
    I
    I have
    I have rhy-
    I have rhythm
    I have rhythm like, etc.
  - Clap on all of syllables that are left out as you proceed through process.
- Challenge students to go through the process again and only clap on the new syllable rather than all of the syllables that are audiated.
  - For example, clap on:
    I
       have
          rhy-
             thm.
- Try each of these processes by lip-syncing the words.
- Stand in a circle and do the exercise in canon, entering 2 beats apart around the circle.
  - Try in it groups of 3 or 4 singers on each part.
  - Challenge students to perform in canon with only 1 person on a part.

General Warm-Ups

Pentatonic Melody

Teaching Ideas

- Sing both of the scale patterns on solfége syllables with hand signs.
- Sing each of the scale patterns in a canon, entering 4 beats apart.
- Sing each of the scale patterns in a canon, entering 2 beats apart.
- Sing each of the scale patterns starting on a different *do*.

Advanced Extensions

- Try singing each of the scale patterns in a canon, entering 1 beat apart.
- Challenge the singers to sing each scale pattern as a canon, entering 1 beat apart with 1 person on each part.
- Sing the scale patterns with different piano accompaniments:
    - Example: march style, waltz, different meters, etc.
- Sing the scale patterns using staccato, legato, crescendo and decrescendo.
- Have all voices sing *pp* in a canon, while one part sings *mf*.
    - Experiment with different dynamic levels on different voice parts.
- Add one or two voices on a single pitch to create a drone affect.

General Warm-Ups

Pat, Clap

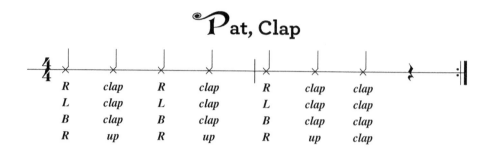

R	clap	R	clap	R	clap	clap
L	clap	L	clap	L	clap	clap
B	clap	B	clap	B	clap	clap
R	up	R	up	R	up	clap

Body Percussion

R = Right hand pat right thigh

L = Left hand pat left thigh

B = Both hands pat both thighs

Clap = Clap hands

Up = Hold left hand flat waist high, bring top of right hand up to touch left palm

Teaching Ideas

- Teach the pat/clap pattern.
- Chant the words with the pat/clap pattern.
- Sing the chorus of *Skip to My Lou* with the pat/clap pattern.
- Sing and pat/clap again in different tempos and dynamics.
- Sing and pat/clap in a canon, entering 2 measures apart.

Advanced Extensions

- Have students create new words to *Skip to My Lou* (page 49) to form a parody.
- Try other songs with the patting/clapping pattern.
  - Have one group sing the chorus to *Cindy* (page 50) with the body percussion.
  - Have the other group sing the chorus to *Skip to My Lou* with the body percussion.
  - Do the same process with *Liza Jane* (page 50).
  - Perform all three songs together.
  - Perform all three songs in a canon at the same.
- Try singing all three songs in different keys at the same time.
  - Example: C Major, E Major and G Major.

General Warm-Ups

Skip to My Lou

Traditional

Fly's in the but - ter - milk, shoo, fly, shoo!

Fly's in the but - ter - milk, shoo, fly, shoo!

Fly's in the but - ter - milk, shoo, fly, shoo!

Skip to my Lou, my dar - ling.

General Warm-Ups

Cindy

Southern Appalachian Folk Song

Get a - long home, Cin - dy, Cin - dy. Get a - long

home, Cin - dy, Cin - dy. Get a - long

home, Cin - dy, Cin - dy. I'll mar - ry you some - day!

Li'l Liza Jane

Traditional

Oh, E - li - za li'l Li - za Jane,

Oh, E - li - za li'l Li - za Jane.

General Warm-Ups

Pepperoni Pizza

Teaching Ideas

- Say the words *pepperoni pizza* like you are really hungry.
- Speak the words in a bored voice.
- Chant the phrase in a sleepy voice.
- Say the words in an excited voice.
- Try the following voices:
  - 3 years old
  - Teacher voice
  - Fish lips
  - Angry
  - Sad
  - Southern accent
  - Witch voice
  - Valley girl (*pepperoni pizza - OMG*)
  - Opera voice
  - British accent
  - Dracula voice
  - Sexy voice (*Hey Baby, pepperoni pizza?*)
- Go around the room and have each student say *pepperoni pizza* in their favorite voice.
  - The class responds by echoing the voice or inflection.

Advanced Extensions

- Go around the room again and have each student say *pepperoni pizza*.
  - Challenge each of them to use a unique voice or inflection, different than everyone else's model.
- Discuss the similarities and differences in the various voices and accents.

General Warm-Ups

What Shall I Do Today?

What shall I do today?

What shall I do today?
What will I sing today?
Why will I smile today?
I feel so good today.
You look so good today.
I love to sing today.
I want to text today.
I want to dance today.
I just love choir today!

Teaching Ideas
- Sing each phrase ascending by half steps.
- Sing the phrase with different tempos.
- Conduct using a fermata over different words of the phrases.
- Sing a phrase over and over, using different word stress or syllable stress with each repetition.

Advanced Extensions
- Change each phrase to a minor key.
- Talk to a neighbor and compare how the message of the text changes when using a minor key.
- Create new phrases and teach them to the class.
- Sing the phrases in various modes:
  - Example: dorian mode, mixolydian mode, etc.
- Rewrite the phrases using synonyms.
  - I want to dance today.
  - Example: Yours truly desires to pirouette this morn.

Inside the Forbidden City, Beijing, China

Great Wall of China

Performance on ancient Chinese instruments, Aiju Elementary School, Shanghai, China

Children at the
Soweto Township,
South Africa

New Africa Theatre
outside Cape Town
South Africa

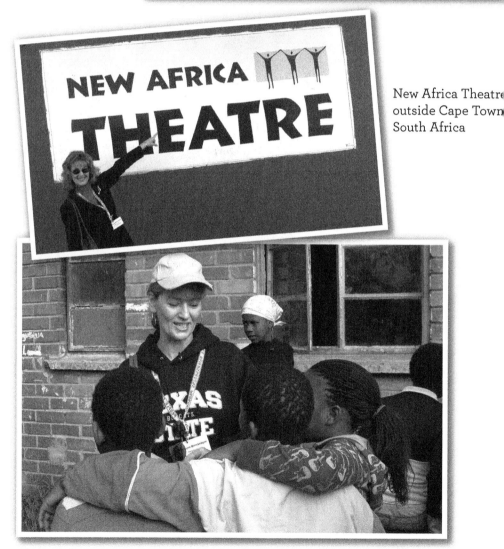

Girls in the Soweto Township, South Africa

Children's theatre at the
Instituto Politécnico,
Havanna, Cuba

Performance by children at
the Project GURI, Indaiatuba,
State of São Paulo, Brazil

Christ the Redeemer statue,
Rio de Janeiro, Brazil

About the Writer

Lynn M. Brinckmeyer

Dr. Lynn M. Brinckmeyer is Professor of Music and Director of Choral Music Education at Texas State University. During 2006-2008 she served as President for The National Association for Music Education (formerly MENC). Past offices include: President for the Northwest Division of MENC, Music Educators Journal Editorial Board, Washington Music Educators Association General Music Curriculum Chair and Conn-Selmer University Advisory Board. She also served as a Music Expert on the Disney, "Let's Play Music" Site. In addition to chairing the Eastern Washington University Music Department for six years and conducting the EWU Concert Choir, Dr. Brinckmeyer received both the PTI Excellence in Teaching Award and the CenturyTel Award for outstanding faculty. Other awards include the MENC Lowell Mason Fellow, Washington Music Educators Association Hall of Fame, the MENC Northwest Division Distinguished Service Award and Eastern New Mexico University's Outstanding Alumni Award.

Dr. Brinckmeyer is a contributing author for *Interactive Music – Powered by Silver Burdett, The Music Director's Cookbook: Creative Recipes for a Successful Program* and *The Choral Director's Cookbook: Insights and Inspired Recipes for Beginners and Experts*. She founded the Eastern Washington University Girls' Chorus while teaching at EWU. She also served as Artistic Director for the Idaho State Children's Chorus in Pocatello, Idaho and the South Hill Children's Chorus in Spokane, Washington. Dr. Brinckmeyer is a co-founder and Artistic Director for the Hill Country Youth Chorus in San Marcos, Texas.

Dr. Brinckmeyer's degrees include a Bachelor of Science in Education and Master of Music Education from Eastern New Mexico University, and a Ph.D. in Music Education from The University of Kansas. In New Mexico she taught elementary music and middle school choir, then moved to higher education in the Pacific Northwest. At Texas State University, Dr. Brinckmeyer teaches graduate and undergraduate courses in choral music education. She serves as Assistant Director for the School of Music and directs the Texas State Women's Choir. Dr. Brinckmeyer has been privileged to lead several music education delegations for People to People and each summer she teaches *Kids, Choir and Drums* workshops for Will Schmid's *World Music Drumming*. She has conducted all state choirs and honor choirs, lectured, presented master classes and performed in forty-eight states in the United States and thirteen different countries, including China, Brazil and South Africa.